Saint Ciaran

Saint Ciaran

The Tale of a Saint of Ireland

by Gary D. Schmidt

Illustrated by Todd Doney

EERDMANS BOOKS FOR YOUNG READERS
Grand Rapids, Michigan / Cambridge, U.K.

For Clare and Jan Walhout, who play by Ciaran's well. — G.S.
To my boys, Reid and Jesse. — T.D.

Text copyright 2000 by Gary D. Schmidt
Illustration copyright 2000 by Todd Doney

Published 2000 by Eerdmans Books for Young Readers
An imprint of Wm. B. Eerdmans Publishing Co.
255 Jefferson Ave. SE
Grand Rapids, Michigan 49503
P.O. Box 103, Cambridge CB3 9PU U.K.

Printed in Hong Kong
05 04 03 02 01 00   7 6 5 4 3 2 1

Library of Congress Cataloging-in-Publication Data
Schmidt, Gary D.
Saint Ciaran: the tale of a saint of Ireland/written by Gary Schmidt; illustrated by Todd Doney.
p. cm.
ISBN 0-8028-5170-3 (cloth : alk. paper)
1. Kieran, Saint, of Ireland. d. ca. 530—Legends. I. Doney, Todd. II. Title.
BR1720.K52S36   1999
270.2'092—dc21
[B]
98-56535
CIP
AC

The Illustrations were done in oils. The text type was set in 13–point Esprit book.
The book was designed by Amy Drinker, Aster Designs.

This story is a true story.

Which is to say it is as true as any story ought to be.

When the folks who live near Saighir hear this tale, they smile a smile and remember.

They remember the well. They remember the fox stopping a moment on dainty paws to sniff

at the stones. Or the doe stepping soundlessly through the bracken, her nose to the night air.

Or in the wilderness darkness beyond, the unblinking yellow eyes of the wolf.

And they hear the wind that breathes over the well, murmuring a name.

Ciaran.

Ciaran's mother Liadain knew that her child was to be no ordinary child. Once, walking beneath a sliver of the moon hooked into the sky, she saw a star fall sparkling. She watched. It did not disappear, but streaked down brighter and brighter and brighter until, when she gasped, it flew into her mouth. She felt the hot glow inside her. And she knew that the star's light would spread over all of dark Ireland.

Liadain birthed her son Ciaran on a day when sunlight mixed itself with the waves shattering against the black rocks of the Isle of Clear. He was as sweet a baby as can be, and as the years trod one upon the other he grew sweeter still. His words were as soft as the green light of a dell, his thoughts as clear as the springs of Corca Laighde, his hands as gentle as the breezes that drew across the island. He spent his days on the shoreline, looking eastward, though he did not know what drew his eyes there.

The animals of Clear trusted Ciaran. Even the badger would let him stroke his sleek sides, and the buck would stoop so that Ciaran might run his hands along its branching antlers.

One bright day, a hawk stretched his talons out of the sky and gripped a tercel dove brooding on her nest. Ciaran cried out for all love, but the hawk pumped its wings and with a screech flew skyward.

Ciaran's tears fell to the sand. He held his hands upward and prayed to a God whose name had never been heard in Ireland.

And the hawk turned. It followed the sea breezes back, and with fierce eyes softened, gently lay the tercel at his feet. Ciaran cupped the bird into his hands, folded her wings neatly to her sides, and looked into her eyes. Laying her back on the nest, he turned to stroke the head of the waiting hawk.

Forever after that day of the world, Ciaran prayed to the God whose name he did not know, and not a day went by without a wonder coming to him. He passed a blackberry thicket in midwinter and berries sprouted into bright reds, then darkened into ripe purples. His feet warmed icy streams, and salmon swam quietly to his hands when he was hungry. At his touch, fire came from rocks, and springs he blessed tasted of wine and honey.

But still Ciaran's eyes looked to the east, and his heart longed for the name of God. And so one spring dawn when the winter storms had passed, Liadain stood on the shore and watched Ciaran wade into the misty sea, his coracle headed to the sun. On the mainland he found passage with a wine merchant, and soon he stood on the prow, parting the foam, salt on his lips, wind weeping his eyes, face always to the east.

They bucked through the choppy waves near the great Gibraltan cliffs, sailed by the parched wastes of North Africa, passed the mountains where Atlas stood holding the sky on his shoulders, and huddled beneath the smoldering mountain of Vesuvius.

And then they came to Rome.

Rome. It rose mountain upon mountain, higher and higher into the sun. When Ciaran entered the city, great bells tolled golden notes. He rushed to the closest church — the first he had ever entered — and the priest was waiting there to baptize him in the name of God.

On the Isle of Clear, Ciaran had found God in the forests and along the shore. Now he found God in the churches. He found God in the psalms he chanted in monastic halls. And he found God in the streets of Rome, where his gentle hand reached warm and healing.

But a day came when Ciaran yearned for the sea breezes of Clear, and on that day he met Patrick, whose eye was as fierce as a hawk's, whose voice was as gentle as a tercel dove's. "I myself will come to Ireland one day," said Patrick, "but you are to go ahead with the name of God in your heart."

Ciaran nodded, his heart quick and glad. "And where in Ireland am I to go?"

"The flowing spring of Saighir. Its water is as clear as clear, as cold as cold, as deep as deep. There you will speak God's name."

"And how is it that I'm to know this spring?"

Patrick handed Ciaran a silent bell. "Until you find Saighir, you'll not hear a sound from it. But at the spring"—and here Patrick smiled—"it will chime like an angel himself was at the ringing."

So Ciaran's eye turned back to the west, his heart carrying the name of God all the while. Through the currents of the Middle Sea, through the stormy channel of Britain, through the trek into Ireland's forests, the bell was silent. Then on a wooded hillside where he could see as far north into Ireland as he could see south, Ciaran found a spring that gushed clear and cold and deep. The bell began to ring with the sweetest tones.

Ciaran knelt down to the spring, cupped his hands into it, and drank. Here he would build his hermitage.

The next morning he began clearing the land for his cell. One by one he cut down the aspens, watching their leafy falls.

When Ciaran came to an oak that sank its roots further down than he could ever hope to dig, Ciaran looked into the woods and his eyes met with a boar's. Slowly, timidly, the boar came into the sunlight. Slowly, timidly, he crossed the clearing. Crouched low, he reached his bristly snout towards Ciaran's outstretched palm. Ciaran scratched him under the chin, and the boar closed his eyes with the pleasure of it.

Then, with fierce grunts and roars, the boar dug up the oak.

Ciaran was never alone after that first day. The bell rang every sweet dawning, and Ciaran would wake to find the boar already at work, furrowing the garden with his tusks.

With rocks the boar rooted up, trees he felled, and mud daubs from the field, Ciaran built his hermitage. He began to pray and sing psalms to the God whose name had never before been heard in Ireland. Every dawning, every noontime, every evening, he would kneel and sing. All the while the boar watched carefully, and when he had finished, Ciaran scratched him under the chin. "Brother Boar, faithful friend."

They were not alone for long.

When Ciaran went to fetch the day's water one morning, he found a doe standing quietly by the spring, her ears up and forward, the white tail high, her black eyes unblinking. Beside her stood a gray wolf, his ears lolling, his tail low but wagging. From behind him, the square snout of a badger looked out. And frisking behind them all, a fox.

Ciaran set his buckets down on the ground. He held his palms out. The doe stepped lightly to him. The wolf bounded and gamboled and whisked his tail in the air. The badger paraded solemnly. And the fox burst from the woods, leapt the stream, and rushed to Ciaran, his tongue hanging from his mouth.

"So," said Ciaran to them all, "I had thought the good Lord made me to be a hermit. But I'm not to be lonely after all."

In time they all came to know their place. After morning prayers, the boar tilled the garden. The doe and badger brought in brushwood, and the wolf dragged fallen trees for firewood. The fox chose the stones for the well Ciaran built around the spring, but mostly he rushed about from chore to chore, helping out where he wasn't needed and glad to do it.

But the wolf still dreamed of hunting herds at night. The boar and badger remembered their fierce and lovely battles. And the fox grew hungry for the taste of meat in his mouth.

One dawn, the fox stole away with Ciaran's leather sandals, gnawing on them deep within the forest. The wolf brought him back, and he came in with his head low, a shy grin across his face. When he lifted a paw to Ciaran's hand, Ciaran could not be harsh. "Well," he said, "perhaps our Lord meant us to walk the earth in bare feet."

Folks who lived by Saighir heard of the animals and came to watch their prayers. When they saw the animals kneel, they began to kneel with them. When they heard Ciaran sing psalms to the name of God, they began to sing with him. And when they saw them all at tasks they did with joy, folks returned home with new hope.

Ciaran built a church, crafting a niche by the altar for the bell. Some who came to watch came to stay, and he built a lodge for them. A monastery grew up beside the well of Saighir, and every dawning, and every noontime, and every evening when Ciaran and the animals knelt down, more and more folk knelt down with them.

Soon so many gathered that they began to ask, "How shall we all eat?"

Ciaran smiled and pointed to the garden. Rows of brown barley, bronze wheat, and golden oats rose higher and fuller than any in all of Ireland. "Watch the wind blow through them," said Ciaran, "and you'll be seeing the breath of God."

"But what of our clothing?" they asked. "Winter draws near."

Ciaran pointed to the woods. A flock of sheep trotted towards them.

As Ciaran grew old, he spent more time alone with his animals, praying. Sometimes his monks would leave him deep in prayer and hear later that he had given communion in Ross Banagher, a three days journey, or that he had been seen at prayer on Cuinche's Rock, far off the coast. But his monks never saw him go.

When Ciaran knew that his last days were come, he called his monks to him. "God has granted me three prayers," he said to them.

"We have only one prayer," they answered.

But Ciaran waved that away. "I asked that there be grace and devotion in Saighir. I asked that all my monks see the gates of heaven. And I asked that all Ireland come to know God's name."

They all wept, even the wolf, who dreamed no longer of anything but Ciaran.

That evening, Ciaran rose and went into the monastery church. His animals stayed behind at the door, holding back the monks. Some said afterwards that Ciaran lit a candle. Others said that light came suddenly from all around the church. But all saw a star streak away from the monastery, back to its bed in the heavens. When the monks took their eyes from the following of it, they saw that the animals had disappeared, that the bell had fallen with no sound from its niche by the altar, and that Ciaran was gone from them.

Over time, stones fell from their mortared places and birches sprang up in the gardens. Memory faded. But some still remember and tell the story. And some still watch, hoping for a sight of the faithful animals on a summer's evening by Ciaran's spring at Saighir.

Author's Note

Of all green Ireland's saints, Ciaran of Saighir was the first. Born on

Cape Clear Island at the very beginning of the sixth century, his first years

were spent in prayer and worship to a God whose name he did not know.

Called to Rome, he traveled the long and dangerous journey to what was

then the center of Christian studies. Sometime around 538, he was ordained

a bishop and sent back to Ireland, encouraged by Saint Patrick, who promised

to follow him. At Saighir, Ciaran lived as a hermit, but soon he gathered to himself

not only a following of animals, but also many monks and nuns.